Camper Van

The incredible story of the retro camper

igloobooks

igloobooks

Published in 2015
by Igloo Books Ltd
Cottage Farm
Sywell
NN6 0BJ
www.igloobooks.com

The measurements used are approximate.

HUN001 0715
2 4 6 8 10 9 7 5 3 1
ISBN 978-1-78440-574-8

Cover image: VW Camper and Commercial Magazine

Printed and manufactured in China

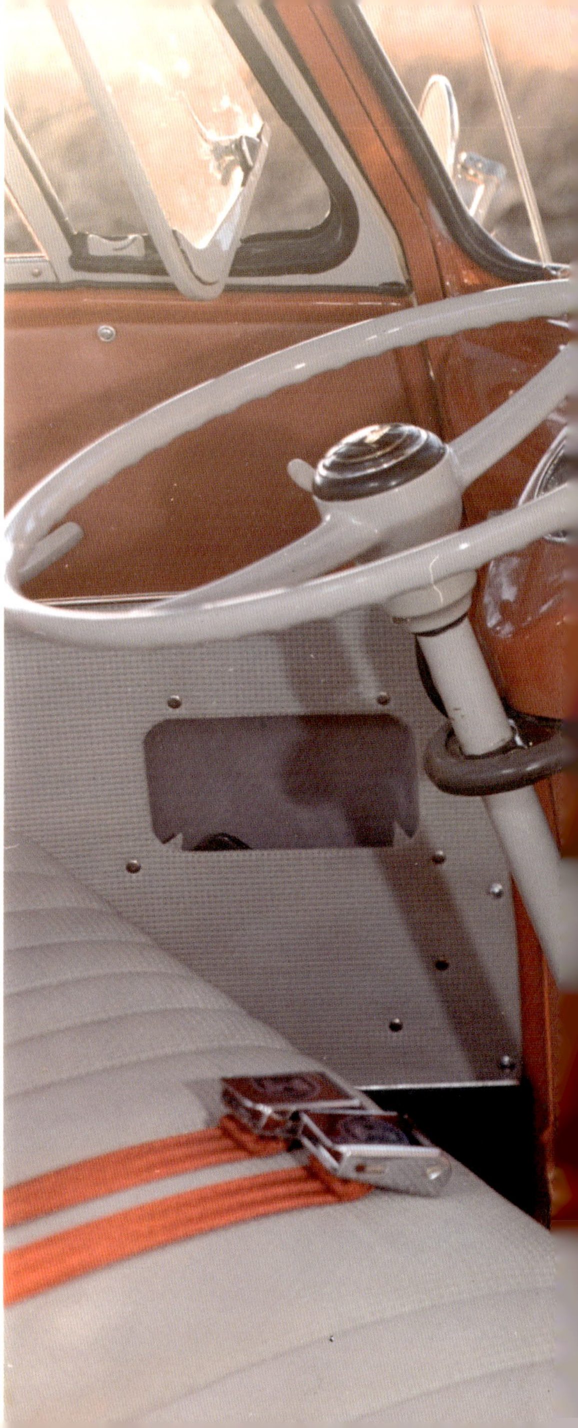

Contents

Introduction

THEY'RE OFTEN BRIGHT, SNAZZY, customised with wacky designs and painted in a variety of colours with a distinctive "rounded" or domed rectangle shape. What are they? VW Camper Vans, of course. Travel to a seaside resort, particularly in the south west of England or a beach in Australia, and you can be guaranteed to spot at least two, if not three or more, of these age-old vehicles in the car park. North America and South Africa also have vast followings of Camper owners and firmly established their own ideologies connected to the vehicle when imports were shipped to both countries during the mid-20th century.

Most often Campers are accompanied by a number of surfboards – visible on the roof rack, if there is one – or sticking up on the seats inside, flung into the back by some exhilarated surfer who's just ridden some awesome waves. But it's not just those who wear wetsuits who opt to travel in Campers; skateboarders and snowboarders are in on the act too. Today, the VW Camper Van is an iconic machine that has stood the test of time and despite the inevitable breakdowns and high maintenance, which is all part of the

◀ Many VW Camper Vans are painted in unusual and colourful designs

fun, the VW Camper Van became a cult symbol of the latter 20th century which looks set to continue as we near the end of the first decade in the new millennium. The Camper is certainly an interesting vehicle on the roads and is a global sensation that has enjoyed a prolific history since the early 1950s.

During the 1950s and 1960s, Camper vans were converted from

▶ Camper Vans are ideal for carrying surfboards down to the beach

the VW Microbus and Plattenwagens as well as Panel Vans, and found favour with many US servicemen who bought them and shipped them from Germany back home. Westfalia became Volkswagen's most well-known converter and maker of the VW Camper Van, as the company, interestingly, didn't go into production for themselves until 2005. They preferred to license other companies including Danbury, Devon, Dormobile and Viking, along with Westfalia Coachworks, to create or convert the Camper based on an original idea by Ben Pon.

The Dutchman, who was a dealer and importer, was introduced to the Plattenwagen at Volkswagen's factory in Germany following the Second World War when demand for a basic vehicle that could be versatile, yet durable, was of the essence in war-ravaged Europe. From Pon's simple sketch came the VW Camper Van which, back in the early 1950s, proved its versatility by becoming a working vehicle, a "before its time people carrier" and the forerunner to the modern day caravan or motorhome by providing families with a second vehicle that could actually take them on holiday – and more than that – give them a dry roof over their heads in the UK's unpredictable summer weather. With Pon's sketch, and the vision and aptitude of Heinz Nordhoff, the VW Camper Van was about to take the world, well certainly parts of it anyway, by storm.

Modern motoring has since become such a serious business. These days it's all about safety, running costs or fuel economy. And don't forget preserving the environment. Do you have the correct kind of child seats? What about side-impact bars and all-round airbags? How bad are your carbon emissions, in fact, are you sure your journey's really necessary? No wonder that there's one little slice of the past that is guaranteed to bring a smile to our faces whenever we see a VW Camper chugging along in the slow lane or labouring up a hill.

Part of it is in the way each and every one is different – whether it's the mismatched replacement panels from a scrapyard somewhere, an incredible custom paint job or the hand-made curtains and upholstery that show just how much their owners love to spend time in them. And you just know there'll be a great history behind it all. It could be nostalgia for youthful travel adventures or bittersweet holiday romances. It could be appalling middle-of-nowhere breakdown sagas that only seem funny when you've arrived home to a hot meal and a long bath and had time to recover your dignity. It could be as simple as summer days on the beach. But every one has its own unique story.

Maybe the VW Camper's appeal is in the way it harks back to a more innocent time of life and a simpler age of motoring – when you were a kid and didn't have to take anything too seriously. When you could fix almost any fault with a bit of common sense and a basic toolkit stored in the back rather than having to surrender your ride to a highly-trained mechanic who's been on a course in diagnostic electronics and has a bewildering array of computers on the workbench. And, pay a fortune for the privilege.

Most important of all, there's that whiff of freedom that we catch whenever we cruise past one of these veterans on the road in our fuel-injected, air-conditioned modern vehicles with their anti-lock brakes and choice of six gears that we hardly know we're driving. It's the idea that we could – if we really wanted to – forget about our jobs, our mortgages, our family commitments and everything that keeps us tied down in one place. And just take off.

The VW Camper reminds us that we are free to see the world, to enjoy a simpler lifestyle that doesn't depend on satellite television, on round-the-clock broadband internet access or all the other gadgets we've convinced ourselves are indispensable. To spend quality time with the people we love, while boiling a kettle on a spirit stove and trying to cook on a single or double ring, doing things that matter to us and seeing sights we'll never forget. To travel where we feel like with no itinerary and sleep wherever we happen to pitch up by the end of the day.

As long as VW Campers are still on the road, we'll secretly know that it could be us out there, doing that. Great, isn't it?

◀ Fully restored post 1965 Camper Van

Chapter 1

History of Volkswagen

▶ Ferdinand Porsche behind the wheel of one of his creations

THE BIRTH OF THE VOLKSWAGEN was perhaps the start of motoring as we know it today – conceived by the famous auto engineer Ferdinand Porsche in Germany from 1931 onwards as the first ever "people's car". Adolf Hitler took a keen interest in its design, demanding that it be made cheap and easy to repair to bring ownership within the reach of the ordinary German citizen. By 1934, the basic shape of what was to become one of the world's most distinctive and best-loved car designs – the Beetle – was in place. A state-run savings scheme was set up to help people buy a Volkswagen but the growing momentum of the Second World War put a stop to its development and its brand-new factory-town known as KdF-Stadt, located in the north of the country, was turned over to making military vehicles and was eventually ruined by heavy Allied bombing.

After the war it was an Englishman who stepped in to save Volkswagen's fortunes. British Army officer Major Ivan Hirst was initially put in charge of salvaging whatever he could from the ruined factories and workshops in the name of war reparations. Instead, finding the British government and motor manufacturers unconvinced of the value of what was essentially Hitler's propagandist auto technology, he set up a workshop to repair British Army vehicles.

It was soon producing new vehicles for the army and for the German Post Office, and Major Hirst, demonstrating a far-sightedness shared by no one else at this time, was responsible for getting the renamed town of Wolfsburg up and running again in order to manufacture the Beetle. He saw to the repair of bomb damage, made arrangements to bring in food for the workers and increased production in the factories. Within two years he had managed to secure tools and machinery, improve the car's design, set up a sales and service network and start exporting the Beetle to the Netherlands.

In 1947 it was decided that a suitable German must be found to take over the running of the company. Major Hirst was instrumental in tracking down and recruiting Heinrich Nordhoff, the former production manager at pre-war motoring giant Opel, who was then working in a Hamburg garage. This was another far-sighted move – Nordhoff headed the company for 20 years until his death in 1968 and was a crucial figure in cementing its success. By the time he took over, at the beginning of 1948, more than 25,000 Beetles had been manufactured at Wolfsburg and the first exports were on their way to America. Within just one year, under

◀ Adolf Hilter admires a model of the Volkswagen car and is amused to find the engine in the boot

▼ An early 1950s convertible Beetle

▲ Beetle cars in production

Nordhoff's leadership, production had doubled. The car was already gaining the beginnings of a cult following in England after some service personnel were allowed to take their Beetles home.

The post-war success of Volkswagen became a byword for German economic regeneration. Nordhoff's recipe was to stick with just the one car model (the Beetle is technically known as the Type 1 and this was the name usually used by Volkswagen) but to work continuously on finding ways to improve the design, to boost the reliability and to increase the efficiency with which it was built. At the same time he turned Volkswagen into a company that German employees were clamouring to work for, with generous pay and benefits up for grabs. Another key decision of Nordhoff's was to put the Type 2 into production in 1950.

Manufactured as a commercial vehicle rather than a car, it was originally based on the Beetle but underwent an extensive improvement process, including wind tunnel tests, that saw it become the prototype for modern vans and passenger vehicles. The Type 2 was the basis for the VW Camper and, as such, it went on to become as iconic in its own way as the Beetle. In 1955 the company set up an American sales and service branch and another company landmark saw a million Volkswagens manufactured and the company developing into a global corporation. Its factories now spanned the globe, with workers in the United States, Canada and Brazil all manufacturing its cars as well as bases in Europe. A luxury sports car, the Karmann Ghia,

▶ Volkswagens ready for export

was marketed by Volkswagen at this time to cater for the upper end of the motoring market and it stayed in production until 1974.

A clever advertising campaign was responsible for successfully positioning Volkswagen as a company that produced cars for the young, fashionable and sophisticated. But despite this, and the iconic status that the Beetle attained, Volkswagen's commercial success actually began to wane during the 1960s. Nordhoff's policy of limiting production to the Type 1 was coming in for increasing criticism. The decade became one of experimentation for Volkswagen, with the Type 3, strongly based on the Type 1's engineering, introduced in 1961, followed by a Type 4 that was a departure from the original design with some major improvements in construction and engineering. But neither was particularly popular and several short-lived models introduced during this period also failed to make much of an impact. In 1964 the company made an important commercial move when it acquired Audi and in 1967 Heinrich Nordhoff announced his intention to retire within a year, making way for a new management style. He was unable to carry this promise out, however, dying within six months of heart failure.

Nordhoff's death was the end of

what had been, on the whole, a hugely successful era at Volkswagen – but a new management style paved the way for new achievements. By the 1970s the "car for the masses" had truly achieved its aim with the Beetle becoming the best-selling car of all time and overtaking the Ford Model T. More than 21 million

▶ A custom made Beetle which featured in the movie 'Austin Powers 2'

models have been sold worldwide. The cars introduced during this decade (often based on Audi designs) secured the future of the manufacturer and are still in production today – the Polo, the Golf (known in the United States as the Rabbit) and the Passat. Inevitably the Beetle, while still enjoying an iconic status around the world, had become a diminishing part of the Volkswagen empire and its production was switched from the Wolfsburg factory to plants in South America. The Golf has remained a mainstay of the company's range with the sporty GTi model introduced in 1985 establishing itself as one of the seminal "hot hatches" and remaining extremely popular to this day.

Towards the end of the 20th century, a time of mergers and consolidation in the automotive industry worldwide, Volkswagen remained a global player, moving its products steadily upmarket and acquiring brands including Skoda, SEAT and Lamborghini. The Czech Skoda brand, formerly a jokey byword for dated Eastern European engineering, was turned around completely after it was acquired by Volkswagen in 1991 when it gained a reputation as a cheap and attractive way to take advantage of superior-quality German engineering. Company brands involved in motorsport include Audi, which has achieved enviable success in rallying and in the Le Mans 24-hour race where it won in 2006 with the first ever diesel-powered car. SEAT competes in the British Touring Car Championship while Skoda is a successful participant in the World Rally Championship.

But the most dramatic and talked-about development from the company in recent years has been the relaunch of the Beetle – attracting acclaim and criticism from enthusiasts in about equal measure. The still-popular Beetle was the natural candidate for a makeover which would bring its engineering, safety standards and the amount of interior space available up to modern standards. The New Beetle was first developed as a concept car after the idea failed to find much favour with Volkswagen management. Public reaction was positive enough to convince the company to put it into production. The car is essentially a re-styled Golf which attempts to capture the "feel" of the classic Beetle while also incorporating futuristic design elements. It has been praised for driveability and reliability

▲ View showing a New Beetle split in two

while being greeted by the motoring press as a car with an appeal based mostly on its looks and styling rather than any outstanding elements to its driving performance. A major break with Beetle tradition is to mount the engine in the front of the car, rather than at the rear, and to move the storage compartment to the back. The relaunch started a trend. The Mini was the next iconic small car to receive this treatment with owners BMW relaunching a modernised version in 2001 and seeing a profits hike as a result. Fiat has recently announced that it intends to do the same with its own baby classic, the tiny but much-loved 500 model. There have also been rumours that the VW Camper is to receive the same treatment as the Beetle but as yet this is unconfirmed.

Recently things have come full circle for Volkswagen with Porsche increasing its stake in the company and appearing to be working towards the goal of complete acquisition of what is already one of its most important partners. Porsche is currently the world's most profitable car maker and the two firms have worked closely together throughout their history. The move, which would finally unite these two manufacturers with a long track record of producing successful cars together, and which were in essence started by the same man, undoubtedly has logic to commend it.

▼ The New Beetle on display

Chapter 2

Ben Pon & Other Key Personnel

▶ Ben Pon with the VW Beetle

THE BEETLE WAS DREAMT UP BY Ferdinand Porsche, then shaped by Major Ivan Hirst and Heinrich Nordhoff. The Type 2 vehicle, eventually to become the VW Transporter, owes its existence to a Dutch businessman named Bernardus (or Ben) Pon who first roughly sketched it out on the page of a notebook during a business meeting in 1947. In the process, though not even a Volkswagen employee, he managed to demonstrate an innate understanding of the company's strengths and to lay the foundations for a second iconic vehicle to go into production. In this way, and also by introducing Volkswagens to America, he helped to secure the firm's success over the next 60 years of automotive manufacture and development.

Based in Utrecht, in the country's central region, Ben Pon set up the first car dealership outside Germany to stock Volkswagen vehicles, in the process building a small family shop into a substantial company which is still in business today. He inherited his business acumen from his father Mijndert Pon, who started the shop in 1895 to supply tobacco, household goods and bicycles to the townspeople of Amersfoort. It expanded into a car dealership and tyre supplier, offering Opel and Ford models during the 1920s. By the 1930s Mijndert's sons Ben and Wijnand were involved in the business and by 1947 they had

turned it into an enterprise that sold around 50 Volkswagens during its first year of operation. They also imported and sold Porsches.

Ben Pon's seminal sketch of what was to become the VW Transporter can easily be viewed by anyone visiting the website of his family firm (www.pon.nl) – now known as Pon Holdings and based in Nijkerk, in the east of the Netherlands. Pon must indeed have had a great deal of empathy with the product

▲ Major Hirst with the Beetle

▶ 1,000th Beetle rolls off the production line in 1946

he was so keen to import. Viewing his drawing reveals what was, for 1947, a strikingly modern piece of automotive design which also captures a good deal of the fluidity that is such a distinguishing feature of the Beetle. It is also striking how recognisable the familiar VW Camper is from this primitive initial sketch. The accompanying story goes as follows: Pon knew he had spotted something great in Volkswagen and was keen to meet the British authorities to negotiate a way of importing the car into his native country. He made an appointment to meet them in the German town of Minden and, while sitting down to thrash out a deal, he pulled out a notebook and drew something that seems commonplace to us now – but for the time was revolutionary.

Pon's big idea was a simple box-shaped delivery vehicle developed from the army utility and factory vehicles that Major Hirst had been producing from the Beetle chassis (known as Plattenwagens). It maximised the space available from the van's footprint, with a driver's cab at the front and an engine mounted centrally at the back. It was also one of the first vehicles in which the driver sat over the front wheels and as such became the prototype for many future vans. The idea of creating a vehicle that could carry more than its own weight in cargo and passengers must have appealed to the Volkswagen representatives present, as within a year Pon was informed that Nordhoff and his technical director Alfred Haesner had decided to press ahead with developing it.

However, they faced a challenging design problem. How to make the box on wheels aerodynamic? For help Haesner

The 1000th VOLKSWAGEN
built during MARCH 1946 coming from Assembly Line

▲ 1948 prototype 1

▶ 1948 prototype 2

visited the University of Braunschweig, which is close to Wolfsburg and a major centre of German technical expertise. There he conducted wind tunnel experiments that resulted in the Transporter having a better aerodynamic performance than the car on which it was based with refinements to its cab area in particular that created a design well ahead of its time. Another problem was the chassis – it needed to be strengthened and the body weight of the Transporter reduced before it could take the strain of a loaded vehicle. The side-loading design meant that cargo weight was distributed more equally between the axles. It took a further three years of development work by Volkswagen designers before all the problems were ironed out and the first Transporters were rolling off the Wolfsburg production line. But after that the vehicle never looked back. Pon's design, although it went through a number of evolutions, remained a fundamental part of the vehicle as late as 1990.

As well as inventing the Type 2 vehicle, and becoming the first ever Volkswagen importer and dealer, Ben Pon is also credited with introducing the marque

to America. In 1949 he travelled to the country in order to research business opportunities and identify a distributor. Accounts differ as to how successful he was on that trip – among enthusiasts legend has it that he had to sell the Volkswagen he brought with him in order to pay his hotel bill – but within 10 years the business was flourishing and half a million vehicles had crossed the Atlantic. It took just two years for this number to double again.

These days, Pon Holdings has more than 9,000 employees in 11 different countries including China, the USA, Belgium, Norway and the UK. The business includes vehicle imports, sales and repairs, oil and gas, heavy equipment such as earth-moving machinery and forklifts and logistics. Commercial vehicles are still part of its operations and in 2007 it is celebrating 60 years of Volkswagen vehicles in the Netherlands. Ben Pon's son, also named Ben, has made a name for himself though not in the area of automobile design. A competitor in the skeet shooting event at the ill-fated 1972 Munich Olympics, he also had a long and colourful career as a racing driver including competing in the 1962 Dutch Grand Prix – albeit briefly; he crashed his Porsche-powered car two laps in and was lucky to avoid serious injury. He also raced six times at Le Mans. He retired in 1965 to concentrate on a career as a vintner and wine importer.

◀ 1950 production line

▼ A converted Volkswagen displaying the diverse uses for the van, even from an early stage

Chapter 3

The Birth of a Legend

▶ A 1949 version of the Microbus

WITHIN THREE YEARS, BEN PON'S back-of-an-envelope idea for a revolutionary cargo-carrying vehicle had been turned into a commercial reality by Volkswagen's designers. The first VW Transporter was unveiled at the Geneva Motor Show in November 1949 – one of Europe's longest-running and most prestigious auto events. The show started out in 1905 and continued uninterrupted during every year between 1923 and the outbreak of the Second World War. When the Type 2 was premiered the show had been revived for just two years and vehicles that appeared for the first time alongside the innovative Volkswagen included a German Borgward Hansa saloon – a big, luxurious family car that must have provided quite a contrast. Other likely exhibitors at this time were Mercedes, Opel and Fiat.

The Type 2 with its 1100cc engine was on the market from March 1950, and it was available in a number of different variants throughout its 40-year lifespan. Like the Beetle, the company stuck with the same basic design but revised it periodically to keep the vehicle up to date and to improve manufacturing efficiency. The Type 2 was eventually issued in five basic variants– the T1 to T5 models, of which the first three variants were substantially based on the Beetle. It is estimated that around five million of these vehicles were made

and sold, and some of the designs acted as the prototype for whole classes of passenger and freight vehicles developed by manufacturers around the world.

The van's low cost and flexibility was the key to its success with the company excellently positioned to take advantage of new business start-ups in the vanguard of economic regeneration following the Second World War. Volkswagen's customers could choose from a variety of styles and usages. The basic model was a delivery van with no side windows and the entire area of internal space behind the front seats available for cargo loading. This was known as the Panel Van and there was also a raised-roof version with even greater space known as the Hochdach. Another popular variation

was the Kombi (an abbreviation of the German Kombinationskraftwagen) which offered removable rear seats and three windows per side for a choice of freight or passenger transport. The Volkswagen Microbus and Deluxe Microbus were an evolution towards the people-carrier and their interiors were designed to be considerably more comfortable and suitable for carrying passengers over longer distances.

The logical next step was a dedicated Camping Van and this evolved, during the vehicle's four-decade lifespan, into a Weekender or Multivan variant which could be used for either regular passenger transport or camping. Following the industrial rather than the passenger path, you could purchase your Type 2 as a flatbed truck with a single or double cab, and with several different load configurations and seating set-ups, again depending on what combinations of cargo and workers you needed to transport. And these were just the vehicles that came out of the Volkswagen factory. The Type 2 lent itself to conversion and experimentation and plenty of mechanics took up the challenge. While perhaps most famous as a Camper, over the years the Type 2 has also been used, among other things, for many different kinds of emergency services vehicles, recovery vehicles, hearses and pickup-trucks. The possibilities are almost endless.

So, how did a utility vehicle designed primarily for post-war industrial use end up becoming a cult legend that is still going strong today? For one thing, it is difficult to overstate

◀ An early 1952 brochure

▼ The changing face of a 1962 VW van

▶ Early Volkswagen vans on the production line in 1953

the originality of Ben Pon's idea. A whole generation of cargo vehicles were born as other auto manufacturers took a look at the Type 2 design and started adapting it for their own purposes. Many of the features we take for granted in vans and cargo vehicles today – a driver's cab over the front wheels, side doors, a loading bay positioned between the front and rear axles, aerodynamic optimisation, even a rear-mounted engine, were pioneered in this vehicle and adapted later by manufacturers as diverse as Ford, Fiat and Chevrolet. In fact, this school of auto design is no longer just the preserve of commercial vehicles. Contemporary car models, centred on the notion of the "people carrier", now incorporate as standard many of the features that Ben Pon first identified in his 1949 sketch, and the concept has spilled over from specialist models into regular saloons, hatchbacks and minis that take advantage of features such as maximum passenger space, sliding side doors and adaptable seating. The curves and fluid lines that have always been one of the most notable features of Volkswagens are now widely fashionable again and the styling pioneered by

the Beetle and the Transporter can today be seen on vehicles produced by manufacturers around the world – one of the factors that created such a positive climate for the development of the New Beetle in 2000.

The Type 2 also flourished commercially thanks to its adaptability. Not only did it come out of the factory in almost any variation you could possibly imagine, but it was also being taken to bits and rebuilt by enthusiastic independent manufacturers who had spotted profitable niches in the market and were keen to fill them. So, whatever you wanted from your Transporter, it was likely that someone could sell you one to do the job. If not, and you were technically-minded yourself, you could probably adapt it – and maybe even sell on your adaptation. The vehicle also benefited from Volkswagen's policy of evolution rather than revolution. While Heinrich Nordhoff eventually attracted criticism for concentrating on the Beetle at the expense of developing new models, his single-mindedness initially meant that huge improvements to performance, reliability and production efficiency were achieved during its lifespan. When it became clear that a major market for the Type 2 would be in passenger vehicles, the company's management philosophy meant that it was easily able to move in this direction.

Volkswagen was also a company of its time, one that took intelligent advantage of the opportunities available to it. Directly after the war, when Germany was initially divided into four

◀ A 1960 Microbus

▼ Heinrich Nordhoff poses in front of his workforce

1 Million Volkswagen-Transporter

◀ One millionth transporter was produced in 1962

zones and moves were afoot to severely limit its steel production and industrial output, the Wolfsburg factory was in the British zone. It was under the control of the Allied power that was most sympathetic to the idea of the nation's economic regeneration and we have already seen the crucial role played by the British Army in its re-establishment as a viable car manufacturer.

By the 1950s, as it became clear that co-operation through trade would be a major building block to securing peace in Europe, it was already developing a network of importers keen to sell its cars across the continent and thus rebuild the reputation of German products. It was also very quick to start exploiting the vast potential of the post-war American auto market. At a time when the disposable income of its customers was low it produced vehicles that were cheap, reliable and economic to run. In fact, Volkswagen managed to make itself a byword for quality auto engineering. And, as the post-war European economy started to boom again, its range of commercial vans fulfilled an important market for other businesses and industries. The stage was truly set for the success of the Type 2.

Chapter 4

Type 2 T1

▶ 1952 Barndoor, an example of the earliest T1 model

THE HIGHLY-COLLECTABLE FIRST generation of the Type 2 Microbus is famous for its distinctive Volkswagen air-cooled engine and split front windscreen and is known with great affection among enthusiasts as the Splittie. This rather basic but extremely characterful vehicle was among the first Volkswagen Transporters to roll off the production line at the Wolfsburg factory during March 1950 and the company continued to produce it for a further 17 years. It was the birth of a whole new motoring era – but it is also very unlikely that those people who watched those first T1s leave the factory realised how important the vehicle was set to become, in both automotive and in cultural terms.

The first T1s were produced at the rate of 10 a day. But demand soon outstripped supply and in 1956 Volkswagen's in-house production was switched to a brand-new Transporter factory in Hanover, staffed by around 5,000 employees. Here the production rate reached around 250 vehicles a day before eventually being discontinued and transferring to Brazil in 1967. There the T1 marque went on to enjoy further modifications and years of success while successive evolutions of the Transporter continued to be produced in Germany. Production of the Camper model was also famously subcontracted to the manufacturer Westfalia from 1951 onwards and a number of other companies were involved in producing variations on the Transporter van from the model's earliest years.

Apart from the split windscreen and a very large engine access door on certain models, distinctive features of the T1 include the large VW logo on the cab front and an impressive cargo capability, including the ability to carry up to eight people, that was unfortunately somewhat compromised by lack of

DAV 3B

SPIELWAREN
W. SCHMIDT
SPIEL-

power, heavy fuel consumption and poor handling. The latter was a consequence of creating a chassis (known as the ladder-frame) that was strong enough to cope with the loading capacity. Another nickname the van attracted was the "Bulli", which is the German for an ox, and this is rumoured to have been considered for a while by Volkswagen as the vehicle's official name before being rejected.

The T1's power came from a flat four-cylinder, rear-mounted, 1.2-litre boxer engine (a term coined to describe a particular movement of the cylinders) which produced 25 horse power although it was upgraded in later Transporters to eventually reach the giddy heights of 40hp. However this version of the engine was not a success and was rapidly discontinued as a result of reliability problems. The power plant, with its distinctive note, was one of the major reasons for Volkswagen prospering as a car manufacturer and its features included cast-iron cylinders, forged connecting rods and crankshaft as well as cast-aluminium pistons and heads. Its air-cooling system used fins on the surface of the cylinders to expose the greatest possible area of the engine to the air that passed across it, rather than relying on a closed water-cooling system and radiator – and this is why rear-mounting it in the Type 2 vehicle was an option.

Three different models of T1 Microbus were produced by Volkswagen between 1950 and 1967. Another important term for T1 enthusiasts was coined to describe the very earliest – the "Barndoor". This often misused nickname, which may possibly be applied more widely than it deserves in a bid to inflate the price of individual vehicles, actually refers to a particular pre-1955 variant, the T1a, which had a very large rear access door for the engine compartment. These vehicles are greatly sought-after by collectors to this day. After 1955 the model's body was slightly modified with a smaller engine bay and access door, smaller wheels and a change to the design of the cab to create the T1b. The last of these three models, the T1c, was in production from 1963 and included modifications to the doors which gave purchasers the options of either a wider rear door as standard or an optional side-mounted sliding door. This model was the last of the T1 vans to be made in Germany before production switched to Brazil in 1967. This led to a distinctive Brazilian

◀ The T1 Microbus was very much the Ford Transit of its day

▶ The Microbus proved the perfect vehicle for firms to advertise their services

model which is known as the T1.5 and which features different styling from the standard models. The Brazilian models are also considered highly collectable among enthusiasts, especially those in America, who also apparently often total up the number of windows to describe their vehicles to each other. The few remaining 23-window Sambas are the most desirable of all buses and, as a result, the most expensive.

An important modification that came along just before the introduction of the T1c beefed up the vehicle considerably – and thus had major implications for the future of the Transporter. In 1962 Volkswagen came up with a model in which the cargo capacity was increased by a quarter – from 750kg to a metric ton. This heavy-duty model also included a more powerful 1.5-litre engine and wheels that were further adapted to carry a heavier load. This soon won favour with customers and led to the rapid discontinuation of the lighter model, thus making the Microbus an even more adaptable and popular option and having a positive effect on the marketability of the T2 marque that was introduced from 1968.

▶ 1954 Coca-Cola delivery Bus

These days, proud Splittie owners and enthusiasts make up a strong part of the classic VW owners' community and are only too keen to share details and pictures of their own beloved vehicles as well as trading information on maintenance and restoration. Prospective owners can access all the help they could possibly need, ranging from manuals and restoration guides to owners' clubs and online communities. These resources provide a wealth of information on T1 ownership including buying tips, advice on preserving bodywork in those climates (including the UK) that are perhaps less sympathetic to classic vehicles, dealing with wiring and electrical problems, maintaining the engine, modifying your Microbus and fixing common faults.

But all this activity only goes to show how desirable and collectable the Splittie, especially the Barndoor model, actually is. These are rare and much-sought-after vehicles that can be difficult to track down. Prospective owners should certainly not expect to be able to pick one up easily or for a bargain price, especially one that is in above-average condition.

TRINK
Coca-Cola
EISKALT
BN 84-6216

Chapter 5

Type 2 T2

▶ 1973
Volkswagen Bay

THE T2, INTRODUCED IN 1968, MADE an immediate and highly-visible break with Microbus tradition by doing away with the split windscreen that was such a trademark feature of its predecessor. This model has therefore become known among enthusiasts as the "bay window" (for obvious reasons) or the "breadloaf" – thanks to its larger size, heavier build and generally blockier shape. Other nicknames around the world included the Kombi and Bulli inherited from its predecessor, and the Rugbrod – a Danish term for a loaf of bread. The appearance is substantially different and the new curved windscreen did actually have considerable benefits for drivers in terms of visibility. Improvements to the bus's cargo capacity and load-carrying ability meant the new model was quite clearly looking towards the future and not the past.

The first T2s went into production in Volkswagen's Hanover factory in Germany. Known as the T2a, these models were equipped with a significantly more powerful 1.6-litre 48hp engine. Major changes had also been made to the vehicle's transmission and suspension. The T1 Microbus had boasted a Beetle-style swing axle at the rear designed to reduce its overall weight, coupled with transfer cases which helped to improve its clearance off the ground. However, this system reduced the vehicle's cornering ability as well as causing potentially dangerous unpredictability in its handling. The new half-shaft axle system that replaced it proved effective in ironing out these handling problems. Four-wheel drive was to be the next transmission development for Volkswagen's technicians to get their

BMW 795L

◀ 1973 Brazilian Fleetline

teeth into, with this innovation first available on the Microbus from the late 1970s.

The T2b was introduced gradually from 1971 onwards and helped to cement the Microbus's continuing popularity with a stream of improvements introduced in Volkswagen's trademark evolutionary style. Production of the bus continued in Germany until 1979 when it was moved first to Mexico and then again, in 1996, to Brazil where the vehicles continued to be popular. It coincided with Volkswagen's attempt to develop a bigger engine for some of its cars – operating in the 1.7 to 2.0-litre range, this new engine was known as the Type 4 simply because this was the Volkswagen model it was intended to serve. While the car did not catch on, the engine was incorporated successfully into the Type 2 Microbus and the more powerful version was available to customers from 1972 onwards, finding particular favour in the North American and Canadian markets where the bus also continued to be a big hit.

With a focus on power and reliability, the inclusion of the Type 4 engine was a big improvement for the

Microbus. The T2b model also featured better brakes and wheels plus a bigger engine compartment and improved air intake vents that were essential to provide the substantial increase in cooling capacity needed by the vehicle when the new engines were on board. In 1973 customers were given the option of automatic transmission for the first time and by 1976 the full-strength 2.0-litre engine was installed and available in the Microbus. Safety was another focus, largely in a bid to satisfy the stringent demands of the American market, and the bus soon had better crash protection from its improved bumpers, plus improved lighting. In 1975 Volkswagen's Hanover factory

▼ Yorkshire water promotional bus

◀ Example of an early Bay (L) and a late Bay (R)

celebrated a major milestone with more than one million Microbuses produced there.

The 1970s were perhaps the true era of the Microbus, with the van playing a large part in the youth movement of this period, representing an anti-materialism, a liberation from social restrictions, sexual freedom and an ability to travel and form relationships with others that were based on something other than the family or workplace – thus greatly broadening the horizons of those involved and striking a blow against traditional race and class attitudes. At this time the Volkswagen logo on the front of the bus was often replaced with a peace symbol and many vans were hand-decorated or given customised paint jobs. The amount of interior space at the driver's command meant the van could comfortably accommodate hitch-hikers, a popular form of transport among members of the 1970s counter-culture and this was seen as another excellent way to meet like-minded people and make new friends.

All things come to an end, and by the

▶ 1968 Devon
▼ 1978 T2 Amescador

late 1970s most aspects of hippy culture had been integrated into the mainstream and the movement had lost much of its impetus. The T2 was replaced by a new model and a very different, more materialistic ethos started to exercise its grip on society. However, this version of the van did not die out. Future developments in the T2 were made for the South American market long after the main focus of Microbus development had turned elsewhere, with the release of a T2c model in 1991. The main differences were more height available in the interior thanks to a raised roof and, from 1996 onwards, a 1.4-litre water-cooled Golf engine featuring in some models, although the traditional air-cooled engine was also used. The use of a water-cooled engine, designed to improve the vehicle's environmental performance, is a major break with Microbus tradition as it is front-mounted and requires a radiator, thereby substantially changing the look of the vehicle.

The T2 is perhaps now regarded by enthusiasts with slightly less affection than the purist's T1 vehicle – but there is no doubt that the improvements introduced by Volkswagen during the 1970s were responsible for considerable gains in safety, reliability and performance. The interior became more spacious and comfortable and the van easier to handle and drive with far more engine power available. Surviving models are often in better condition than the ageing T1s and easier to maintain and source parts for. All in all, the T2 may represent a good compromise these days for a prospective buyer looking for an authentic slab of Microbus history and a reasonable degree of comfort and safety. Models are widely available and can be bought extremely cheaply, although the condition of such vehicles is an important consideration.

Chapter 6

Type 2 T3

THE T3, INTRODUCED FROM 1979 onwards, can just about be called a next-generation development of the Microbus and therefore remains an example of Volkswagen's original evolution-not-revolution policy towards developing its vehicles. It was, however, a clear attempt to break with the past and to position the bus as a modern vehicle. It is the last of the rear-engined buses and the last to be developed in this evolutionary way, and it shows considerable differences from its predecessors. During this period the company itself was recovering from an earlier crisis in its fortunes that had been narrowly averted by a new management style and the introduction of a far wider range of vehicle models, many of them inherited from Audi, a company it had bought a few years previously. Rather than a range with austere titles like the "Type 1" and "Type 2" it was now

◀ T25 Aircool

marketing cars with familiar names like the Golf, Polo and Passat. It was inevitable that the change of focus at Volkswagen and its attempts to bring itself up-to-date as a modern motor manufacturer would be reflected in one of its most successful products.

The T3 Microbus was, however,

◀ T25 Caravelle

available in a wide range of models just like its predecessors – as a passenger van and as different types of Camper, for example. It had continued to be customised by manufacturers such as Westfalia. It is known by many different names in different parts of the world. To the British and Irish it was the T25 or the Caravelle, while Americans and Canadians called it the Vanagon (a portmanteau word created from van and wagon) and this model featured certain developments necessary to market it in those countries. Introduced from 1980 onwards, the bus continued the trend of maximising the space available with the inclusion of a wider body, a repositioned engine compartment and a larger rear door giving far superior access to the interior. However its appearance was now much squarer and blockier, having lost the rounded, fluid lines that were such a feature of the earlier vans, with the likeliest design imperative being to meet modern crash protection standards as well as signalling a clear break with the past.

The T3 was also considerably heavier and was at first felt by some to be underpowered for its size and weight. For the first years of T3 production a similar range of air-cooled engines as had powered the T2 was on offer, starting at a somewhat flimsy 1.6 litres. But from 1982 onwards various engine modifications were introduced bringing the available capacity as high as 2.1 litres. The vehicle switched over to water-cooling with the introduction of the Wasserboxer for the US market in 1983, an engine developed especially by Volkswagen for this model and never used anywhere else. A diesel engine was also made available and from 1985 onwards a Syncro option with four-wheel drive became a purchasing possibility.

The Wasserboxer was a departure for Volkswagen and, as with so many developments in automotive technology at this time, emissions legislation was responsible. These strict laws had a particular impact on European vehicles heading for the crucially important American market and were responsible for a significant loss of performance in many British sports cars which sacrificed a major reduction in power for compliance with the rules (sometimes sufficient to terminally damage the desirability of the car). Manufacturers

▶ 1990 Westfalia Atlantic

that got the American market wrong tended to suffer badly over the next couple of decades, so there was a lot at stake.

The Wasserboxer engine had an innovative design that did away with a timing belt and also modified the way that the cylinders were constructed. However, design issues led to some reliability problems, especially with the cooling system. Head gasket failure and even entire engine failure were also not uncommon. Modern buyers of models from this era are regularly advised by other enthusiasts to pay particular attention to head gasket leaks and problems with the cooling system.

Volkswagen had attempted to address power and emissions issues with its engine developments – but what about features and driveability? In this respect the T3 was undoubtedly of a different generation from its predecessors with passenger safety and comfort much improved. The model boasted better brakes, power steering and the kind of equipment that was starting to be viewed as standard on most cars – such as central locking and heated mirrors. Air conditioning was also offered – but of a rather unconventional type which left a lot of ugly ductwork inside the vehicle. It was eventually improved by Volkswagen but remained one of the more problematic features for vehicles of this era. Other quirks included reliability issues with the manual transmission in early models and unconventional locations for some parts that require maintenance, such as a brake fluid reservoir behind the dashboard and a battery under the passenger seat.

The last T3s were built for the European market in 1989 with the T4 being introduced in 1990. However a few four-wheel drive and much sought-after limited-edition models were produced in Germany and Austria in the early 1990s and vehicles were also manufactured for the German Post Office. The T3 lived on until 2002 in South Africa where it was known as the Volksie Bus and it continued to be produced with a modified body, fuel injection and a more powerful engine, including a five-cylinder Audi model used in some vehicles.

The T3 had ensured that the Microbus survived into the next era of motoring as a modern and practical utility vehicle – and shed the “summer

of love" associations that perhaps by now would have threatened its marketability – but at great cost to its distinctiveness and character.

In retrospect, it is quite possible to see how Volkswagen's canny repositioning of the van paved the way for many of the developments in car design that dominated the next two decades. But, to all those enthusiasts and collectors of the Splittie and Bay models, the T3 must truly have seemed like the end of an era.

Chapter 7

T4 Eurovan

▶ T4 Eurovan Camper conversion

IN 1990, A COMPLETELY NEW concept arrived in the T4 which was a modern four-berth alternative to the older and out-dated (at the time) Type 2 model. Although slightly more boxy in shape than their predecessors, the T4 came in a small, compact version with its engine placed at the front of the vehicle for the first time in the history of VW Camper Van's history. They were a sophisticated motor caravan which spanked of reliability in the way that the T2 had done before, and came equipped with microwaves, ovens, showers, satellite navigation as well as a television and CD/DVD players – although these admittedly came later.

With their turbodiesel engines, these vehicles were much better on driving reliability than their forerunners and introduced the driver to power steering, servo brakes, five-speed gearboxes and modern heating – which proved to be a world away from the Devons, Vikings, Dormobiles and other conversions of the mid 1960s onwards. The T4 was quickly snapped up by both domestic purchasers and those wishing to travel across Europe in style – yet with all the charm and flamboyance of the Campers that had set the scene for VW camping some 20 or so years before.

All were equipped with electric hook-up (even though many camping sites had yet to catch on) and were defined by their standard crockery, cutlery, cycle rack and extra table to make the home-away-from-home experience just that bit more alluring to potential buyers. A free-standing awning (or tent) was also often part of the deal and those wanting to brave the elements were convinced by this all-singing, all-dancing alternative to the earlier VW Camper conversions.

However, despite all the trappings, many advocates of the older-type

conversions thought that the charm and appeal was lost in this modern alternative and that the flight to freedom was not quite as fancy free as it had been and still could be in an older type vehicle. But Volkswagen had been thinking about updating their trusted conversions for some time. In fact, as early as the late

▶ T4 Eurovan Transporter TDI

1970s plans were on the horizon for a more modern-day equivalent to the T2 model. They wanted a front engine which would come with a water-cooled design as had already taken place with VW cars sometime earlier in the 1970s. The overheating problems with engines encased in the rear were not helping the VW reliability image and something needed to be done.

In 1980, the company's answer was the T3/Vanagon which still advocated a rear engine and it is thought that company politics played a large part in this decision to continue with a boxer engine. It would be 10 more years before the T4 would hit the roads and it was VW's first Transporter without a boxer engine (i.e. it was housed in the front). The T4 was a front-wheel drive model that came on two wheelbases which gave it a great deal of flexibility from three-axled minibuses to large boxed ambulances and had transversely-mounted engines with four, five and six cylinders and a TDI diesel engine – which was a great asset at the time.

The Eurovan, as the T4 Camper was known, was state-of-the-art, which was more than could be said for the T2, and as a result the new innovation became a huge success. The last T4 models left the production line in 2003 after no less than 14 years in service although there were rumours that the Chinese market was keen to keep the fire burning as far as the T4 was concerned.

There was only ever one major change to the T4 which took place in 1994 when the re-shaped front end was introduced as a necessity to accommodate the six VR6 cylinder engine. The two "hybrids" that emerged as a result were named the T4a and T4b by VW enthusiasts and the Eurovan really took off in the US as passenger versions from Europe became highly sought-after exports. Many were then sent to US firms for conversion, particularly to Winnebago Industries and Rialtas who then sold the conversions to Winnebago dealers direct.

The Eurovan Camper was a long wheelbase commercial van that was mainly converted by Winnebago Industries and included a pop top roof with two double beds and seating for four. There were also optional single or two people centre seats with two, four-people tables and two bucket seats which were designed to be swivelled to face the dinette and kitchen area.

DAYTONA
P543 TWL

Chapter 8

Type T5

▶ T5 California

LIKE THE T4, THE T5 WAS AN innovative Transporter which was rife for conversion, and its arrival in 2004 came some 14 years after its predecessor. As a commercial range the T5 is a substantial transport machine which became incredibly important in the market place in Europe. The reason for this seems to have been its versatility including the Panel Van – which is manufactured without side windows or rear seats and the Highroof Panel Van which also comes in an optional extra high roof – in all there are three roof heights available on this van. It has also been designed on the Kombi with side windows and removable rear seats as well as acting as both a passenger and loading vehicle which can also come with a higher roof.

The T5 also comes in a Half-panel

▶ The Microbus throughout the decades

design meaning that it has side windows in the front half only and one row of removable seats, yet it also comes as a flatbed truck with a wider load bed as well as a combination of double cab and two rows of seating. It also hails as a flatbed truck with lowered load bed and a naked chassis with a cab which is designed for coachbuilders to do what they will to customise the vehicle to their own specifications. But, there are also a number of other conversions available, many of which are offered through VW dealerships. These comprise ambulances, police vans, ladder trucks, refrigerated vans and fire engines to name but a few.

But the T5 is not only an MPV for the commercial and private sector. It is also an MPV that offers a competitive lifestyle range for the discerning traveller or family. The Transporter, as it's known in Europe, where it's also called the Shuttle or Kombi, is a "Van" that can comfortably seat up to nine people whereas the Caravelle or Multivan, which is one step up from the basic T5, comes as a seven-seater which has a number of options available so that seating can be arranged in the best positions for the passengers on board.

There is a clever rail that runs around the vehicle and allows a combination of seating arrangements as the accessories fit onto the rail to allow flexibility.

The final models in the range are the Campers which include the Kombi/Multivan Beach and the California which are all conversions of the new T5 model.

The Kombi/Multivan Beach has a foldout bed while the California is more of a traditional Camper Van with beds and other facilities such as benches or seats, tables and a sink. The T5 was voted International Van of the Year in its year of arrival and was voted the following year, in 2005, as Australia's Delivery Van of the Year. In 2006 the Australians once again gave the VW T5 this accolade and its versatility is still proven in both the northern and southern hemisphere today.

A new VW Camper that was converted in the late 1960s would have cost between £850–£1,300 depending on options. A T5 in today's environment will set the purchaser back by over £21,000. In 2006, the new Kombi Beach was launched in Australia and although many were enthralled with their new purchase, other previous owners of VW Camper Vans thought that the new edition was a pricey bed on wheels. However, despite some criticism for its industrial look and expensive outlay, the Camper remains a firm favourite with the fraternities with which it has become

◀ Future of the Camper Van

synonymous, including those seeking freedom and the waves. No one seems to want friends to write on the inner walls anymore, and the basic camping is gone with the hi-tech facilities on board. Nevertheless, the T5 still offers the chance to get away from it all and live the dream that is undoubtedly still etched on the minds of many.

Chapter 9

Dormobile

▶ 1972 Dormobile

VOLKSWAGEN'S TYPE 2 VEHICLE was a completely new and very popular concept. As a result demand was very strong, and led to a number of companies spotting a profitable niche market. Soon these companies were offering conversions of Type 2s into specialist models such as Camper Vans. While Westfalia was the official Volkswagen partner in this enterprise, Dormobile is one British company that also provided a Camper conversion for the Type 2, offering both factory conversions and conversion kits. It would install prefabricated parts, such as seats that converted to beds, or lifting canvas roofs, or even a complete caravan interior with a simple strengthening of the base of the vehicle in order to support the additional weight on the roof. Dormobile would even fabricate parts especially for individual requirements and each conversion was identified with a special riveted-on identity tag. As a result, a practically infinite variety of Dormobile conversions were available for almost any suitable vehicle and the company has become a byword for the motor-caravanning experience.

More properly known as Martin-Walter Ltd, the Kent-based firm had a long and prestigious history as a coachbuilder stretching back into the 18th century. As the era of the motor car dawned it kept apace with the industry and provided coachwork for prestigious brands such as Mercedes Benz, Daimler and Rolls-Royce. But the camping boom that started in the early 1950s and lasted for at least a decade caused a change of focus. The Dormobile name was born, becoming one of the most powerful influences on the British love of motorised

VRB
726 K

camping, because of the cheap and accessible alternative it offered to the conventional towing caravan. These years saw a big increase in the number of people attracted to this kind of holiday and the company worked with a wide range of manufacturers, not just Volkswagen. Its first conversion was based on a Ford chassis and its Bedford van conversion (based on a Vauxhall model) was a very common sight on British roads from the 1950s onwards.

The Dormobile conversion for the Volkswagen bus was popular because of its distinctive side-lifting roof, with its often colourful canvas fitted section, which offered an unprecedented eight feet of standing room – more than enough for the tallest Camper. This literally opened up the van to all kinds of possibilities, including stacking bunks and extra child beds. Other amenities available to Volkswagen Dormobile drivers and their families included up to three gallons of water storage, a wardrobe and a cooker. Many were equipped with decorative curtains and upholstery as well as inspiring the custom paint jobs that have always been such an integral part of all Volkswagen Type 2 ownership.

This cheap and practical conversion brought motor caravanning within reach of a whole new group of enthusiastic holidaymakers and before many years had passed the secondhand Dormobile bus also became extremely attractive to young travellers wanting to take a budget trip with friends – a trend that is still going strong today, especially among surfing enthusiasts in the south west of England.

But life moved on, as it always does, and by the late 1960s demand for Dormobile conversions was decreasing – not least because of the introduction of cheaper standalone caravan models like the iconic Sprite and the increasing popularity of foreign travel. This led to the company switching its focus again, this time away from camping and onto building its own range of small and medium-sized buses. Very few conversions were carried out after 1970 and the company ceased trading altogether in 1994.

These days the Dormobile would certainly have trouble competing with the huge, luxurious motor homes,

◀▼ Promotional photos illustrating the lifestyle of the Camper Van

▶ T3 Dormobile Conversion

featuring every amenity from electricity, running water and bike storage, to satellite television, microwaves, fixed double beds and flushing toilets, that are routinely seen lumbering around the highways of Europe and the US and taking up acres of prime location at campsites. But in their time they were a genuine innovation and their enduring popularity has ensured that such vans do stay on the road and still make their appearance

in holiday hotspots – bringing a smile to the face of many people as they do so, who maybe can't help wishing, for a moment, that they were on board. Dormobile-converted Volkswagen buses are still keenly traded secondhand and plenty of small-scale entrepreneurs have also stepped in to provide enthusiasts with replacement accessories.

Chapter 10

Riviera

▶ A 1978 Riviera

CONVERSION TO THE VW MICROBUS is distinctive for its side-lifting roof with canvas sleeve, the "pop top" look is a product of the ASI Riviera conversion popular in the United States. This consists of a central fibreglass roof panel supported by crossed struts that can be pushed straight upwards to provide valuable extra space in the middle section of the vehicle. Different roof panel sizes as well as fixed-headroom models were on offer, some including storage or even extra sleeping accommodation. And, as with the Dormobile, a canvas section usually linked the lifting roof to the body of the van. The conversion deal included all interior fixtures and fittings.

The Riviera will forever be associated with America's Pacific North West region. Automotive Services Incorporated (ASI) was a motor company based in Washington State that got together with a dealership called Riviera Motors from neighbouring Oregon. The partnership was formed to satisfy the voracious local demand for Volkswagen Camper conversions. So popular was the officially-sanctioned Westfalia van that there simply weren't enough vehicles on sale and prices had gone through the roof. As a result Riviera asked ASI to help it with an alternative Camper conversion for the T2 and T3 models of Volkswagen Transporters – which could be easily obtained thanks to Volkswagen's policy of forcing Westfalia importers to accept other models as part of their order. The new product was marketed under the name of "Campwagen".

The Campwagens were available from the mid-1970s onward, named the Riviera Line, and sold under the

slogan: "The Camper with the heart of a Volkswagen" (later "The Camper with the heart of a Vanagon"). Its sales brochure pictures a range of converted Microbuses parked below scenic mountain peaks and on peaceful lake shores and its occupants (mainly families and older couples) are shown enjoying meals in the well-appointed interior or even tucked up cosily in bed. As well as offering the "pop top" there were a selection of raised fixed-headroom roofs that bolted onto the existing Volkswagen Transporter range, providing extra space and, in some cases, light and ventilation

LFW 59N

through integral extra windows.

Models included the Vista, the Penthouse and the Plan I with standard equipment including a two-burner propane stove, foam mattresses with stain-resistant covers, wall-to-wall carpets, a linen closet, a cutlery drawer and colour-co-ordinated curtains. Marketing focused on the cosy accommodation and generous storage space inside the vehicle and optional extras included air conditioning, a stereo system and an awning. You could fit an icebox or an odour-free chemical toilet to your Campwagen and even sling a hammock under the pop top for a child to sleep in. A healthy competition developed between Westfalia and ASI over the Volkswagen conversion market and features developed for one vehicle could often be seen popping up in the other within a fairly short timescale.

The Volkswagen Camper is held to be synonymous with the Californian surfer lifestyle to be found on America's west coast. But the Pacific North West region, a little to the north of California, also has its own long and passionate tradition of Microbus ownership that owes a lot to the area's spectacular mountain scenery and breathtaking natural beauty (although its notoriously damp and rainy climate probably does little for the vehicles' bodywork). Some wonderful locations to visit with your Camper include cosmopolitan Seattle and friendly Portland, the Cascade mountain range, one of America's most active volcanic regions that includes the recently-erupted Mount St Helens, Puget Sound and the San Juan Islands, the arctic Mount Ranier National Park or the spectacular Columbia River gorge. With all this natural beauty to enjoy, and the delights of Canada just across the border, no wonder that getting back to nature with the help of your Camper Van still seems like such a good way to spend time.

There are many clubs and enthusiast groups catering to this specific region and several companies offering drive-yourself touring holidays in fully-restored Westfalia and Riviera Camper Vans. The connection is so strong that it is fair to say a journey through Oregon and Washington State to Vancouver counts as one of the classic American road trips – and is an experience that should warm the heart of all Volkswagen Camper enthusiasts.

◀ An imported Camper

Chapter 11

Sundial

▶ Sundial brochure featuring a T1 conversion

THE SUNDIAL CONVERSION WAS another product of the North American sales boom that had made the Westfalia dedicated Camper model almost impossible to buy new in that country – especially since that company's production figures were never particularly high in the first place, with around 1,000 vans coming out of its German factory in the space of seven years. Other Volkswagen Transporter models, in comparison, were so easily available that dealers sometimes had problems in shifting them off the forecourt – the result of a calculated policy by Volkswagen to only offer Westfalia vans to importers who were prepared to take consignments of its other models. It can be imagined that this was a cause of considerable dissatisfaction with the manufacturer, and people, as so often happens, started to look for a way around this problem.

The Sundial project, therefore, had a very simple and entrepreneurial basis: to get hold of these easily available Volkswagen Type 2 Panel Van or sometimes the Kombi model, and to turn it into a much more desirable and highly sought-after Camper Van equipped to sleep six people. Dealers, especially on the West Coast of the United States and in Canada, were clamouring for more Volkswagen-based campers and Sundial created a straightforward, no-frills product to fill that need.

Sundial models were popular in the US and Canada and vehicles with these conversions tend to date from the mid-1960s onwards which means the adaptations took place on T1 split-windscreen models that are now highly desirable to collectors. Plenty are offered for sale however would-be

sundial camper

owners should exercise caution before buying. It can sometimes be hard to tell whether a particular Volkswagen Camper truly is the product of a Sundial conversion, rather than actually being a one-off or an item from one of the myriad small companies in Britain, America and elsewhere that were busily converting similar vans.

It may be possible to check a vehicle's serial number against lists compiled by enthusiasts and to work out how it started out in life – this could provide a clue since the company worked mainly with panel vans. Most Sundials are very obviously converted vans, and

▼ Sundial VW Camper

this has tended to polarise opinions among enthusiasts. Some feel this conversion impairs their attractiveness and collectability, while others have a great affection for them for exactly this reason. The vehicles had hinged double doors which opened outwards on the passenger side, and generally featured a raised-height fibreglass roof panel that often contained extra windows.

One way to identify a Sundial is its three small windows per side which do not occupy the whole of the van's length, although on some models this may be reduced to two on the driver's side. They tend to be push-open but some are louvre windows, reminiscent of the type Westfalia used. All this can make tracking down the exact pedigree of a particular van rather difficult since parts did not tend to be unique to a particular conversion company. However Sundial did put a distinctive badge bearing the company logo into many

◀ 1967 Camper with hinged double doors

of its conversions and this is the surest method of identifying the company's work – however, reproductions of these are available too. The original spare wheel cover also carried the company logo. The interior was finished throughout in vinyl and could be carpeted as an optional extra. It featured a forwards-facing seat that folded down into a bed, plus a table and storage cupboards. It is very easy to imagine how, if the manufacturer's claim to sleep six was actually fulfilled, it might have got rather crowded in there.

One bit of Sundial equipment has made it into the annals of Volkswagen Camper folklore almost to a greater extent than the vehicle itself. This is the awning that it produced to shield the area around the side doors from the elements. Supported from the vehicle on poles, and with drop-down sides that allowed its conversion from a canopy to an all-enveloping tent, it was often made from a particularly vivid green and white stripy fabric and is now regarded as a collectors' item in its own right – not least because it is adaptable for use with other models. Where original Sundial awnings exist today they often come with replacement poles due to the stresses and strains the originals had to take.

Chapter 12

Westfalia

▶ A classic 1959 advertisement featuring a Westfalia conversion

TODAY ONE OF THE MOST collectable Volkswagen Type 2 vehicles in existence is a T1 that has been treated to a Westfalia camping conversion.

That said, any Westphalia-converted Volkswagen was like gold dust from the moment the company started sub-contracting their manufacture. The vehicles were immediately snapped up out of the hands of any dealer lucky to get a supply, especially in the North American market in the mid-to-late 1960s and early 1970s. Dealers recall customers queuing around the block just to get a look inside the Westfalia Van and being prepared to take any available model, regardless of colour.

Its official status and great popularity means that Westfalia has become synonymous with Volkswagen Campers, despite the fact it was one of nearly 40 companies carrying out such conversions. However the Westfalia Camper remains a

HE VOLKSWAGEN CAMPER
WITH WESTFALIA DE LUXE EQUIPMENT

UOA 459L

A 1973 Westfalia

standout favourite with enthusiasts, earning itself the affectionate nickname Westy.

The Campers were, just like Volkswagen's home-grown products, made available exclusively from company dealers around the world. It also set up a tourist delivery programme which allowed a new owner to collect their vehicle fresh from the factory and take it on a leisurely drive home. This is an option still offered by luxury car makers today, notably Mercedes Benz, out of consideration for purchasers that want to be the only people to have ever driven their dream car.

And the van produced another interesting social phenomenon stemming from the sheer numbers of US troops stationed in Germany for many years after the Second World War had ended. Lots of services personnel bought up Volkswagen Campers to take back home, thus greatly stimulating interest in the vehicle in that country and, perhaps, contributing to the explosion of interest in conversions described above.

The Westfalia production works was based at Rheda-Wiedenbrück in the north west of Germany – about 150 kilometres from Wolfsburg and Volkswagen's home base. It, like the Volkswagen factory itself,

◀ Volkswagen advertising featuring a Westfalia conversion

was located in what had been the British zone in the post-war period where a slightly more sympathetic attitude to the reconstruction of German industry prevailed. Its adaptation of the Type 2 into the official Volkswagen Camper started in the early 1950s with the T1 and it continued for more than 50 years covering many models and offering a vast array of different options and extras. It is estimated that between 1951 and 1958 around 1,000 conversions were carried out until, in August 1958, a series of new versions were introduced known as the Sonderausführung or Special. These were numbered with a SO-prefix from that point onwards depending on their year of manufacture.

What could a purchaser climbing aboard their brand-new Westfalia expect to find? The Volkswagen most commonly adapted was the Kombi, the van that featured side windows and removable rear seats. Standard equipment on the converted vehicle included a folding table, various different options for converting the seats into beds, cabinets, cold storage (either an ice-box or a cold-box) and arrangements for water storage. Some models had sinks and an electrical hook-up. Interior décor included wood panelling, curtains and window screens. Add-ons varied between improvements to the van's driving comfort and its living accommodation. If the former was your main concern you might have chosen from an automatic transmission, air conditioning and a map table. If the latter was your priority a variety of tents and awnings, cots for children, a camping stove or a chemical toilet may have seemed more important.

It is important to remember that Volkswagen never issued a dedicated factory-based Camper model so the Westfalia is the nearest to a purist vehicle in this class that it is possible to get. Conversions were still being carried out as late as 2003 and today identifying these highly-collectable vans is an important matter so it is useful to understand how they were categorised at the factory. From 1958 onwards, at the introduction of the SO- models, a square plate was attached into the vehicle using two rivets or screws giving its date of manufacture, its serial number, model number, paint finish and export information as well as any additional options that were included. These plates contain data known as an M-code and, if intact, they can be located behind the right-hand front seat. Anyone wanting more help in understanding this, or seeking advice on Westfalia reconstruction, ownership or purchase will find a wealth of resources to help them including websites, books and collectors' clubs.

◀ 1969 Westfalia

Chapter 13

Devon

▶ 1967 Devon Conversion

RENOWNED FOR ITS HIGH QUALITY and oak woodwork, the Devon was one of the UK's most famous conversions and the company was one of the few converters officially licensed by VW. During the 1960s and 1970s, nothing else surpassed the Devon which came with a warranty guaranteed by VW. Between 1957 and the following decade, there were two businesses that were instrumental in making the Devon a phenomenon in the UK with after-sales servicing. These comprised JP White (of Sidmouth, Devon), who were prolific in their cabinet making, and Lisburne Garages, who were responsible for producing a motorhome based on the VW Camper as well as working in sales and distribution.

By the following year, the Devon was ready to take to the roads and was finished in solid light oak. It featured a table and bench dinette which could be converted to a double bed by taking down the table between the benches. Seating was provided by foam which was four inches thick and covered in washable covers. These also doubled as mattresses at night time when the curtains – which fitted on slide runners – could be pulled around the windows for privacy. There was also a two-burner gas cooker and a storage area in the guise of a cabinet that provided those home-from-home comforts. Just behind the engine area there was additional storage while gas was used outside the vehicle to encompass safety regulations. As in line with motorhomes and caravans of today, an awning extension was available. Although, unlike its modern successors, these awnings resembled more of a canopy than an additional space outside the main vehicle and were available with, or without, side extensions.

The table which sat snug in the dinette could also be used as a stand-alone item outside the vehicle. They were continually advertised as a convenient holiday home

that travelled with the family as well as being a pre-requisite for the commercial businessman who needed a bed for the night. Early Devons were seen as a luxury and sold for in excess of £800 which at the time was a great deal of money to part with if it was only used for a two-week holiday each summer. Of course, costs could spiral when an awning or roof rack were optional extras that were a must-have for the would-be "second home-owners". When the Devon made its debut at the Caravan and Boat Show at Earl's Court, there were three models available.

The Mark I was a budget model whereas the Mark II came complete with a water tank and pump tap which was much like other caravans of the era. These pump taps were located in the floor and required the user to continually pump water, with their foot on a rubber pad. However, the Mark III was aimed at a different audience entirely and was out to glean sales from the commercial market.

Advertised as the Devon Caravette and focused on the market of "Gentlemen of the Road" – the people today we call reps – the Mark III had those extras including a

DEVON

◀ 1959 Devon Samba

table fixed to the bulkhead so that owners could work while seated at the long bench. It doubled as a single bed which could also be extended to cater for family weekends or holidays if needs be. It also comprised a filing or storage space under the bench seat in the form of a cabinet and had an open fronted wardrobe near the rear. It was the quintessential workplace and office and afforded those who were working away from home the facilities to cater for clients while on the road. One important part of the Devon's commercial advertising campaign was its ability to be self-sufficient and on "home territory" as it were, without the need for finding accommodation at short notice. Despite its revolutionary stance in the business world, the life of the Mark III was short-lived and today there are no known surviving models to be found anywhere in the world.

▶ 1978 Devon brochure

In 1959 with the Mark III all but abandoned the Devon continued to develop as a camping vehicle. Modifications were made and by 1960 the company introduced a new Caravette which in part reneged on the previous quality. Some of the most useful units were replaced and others let go altogether. Squarer units which had less appeal in terms of craftsmanship were overruled in favour of more versatile units that appeared less attractive. The company JP White who had become synonymous with the workmanship of the Devon suddenly became integral in the new Caravette as well as contributing to other conversions such as the Austin 152. All Devons now comprised accommodation for two adults and two children and a new 50-litre water tank was introduced as standard while the small wardrobe was still contained in the bulkhead. In addition, the fuel tank was now housed within the vehicle in the engine bay while the seating favoured what was described as "deep foam" in its upholstery. Two years later and the fully functioning Devonette was the new "kid" on the block.

The Devonette was introduced as another budget version of a camping vehicle and was based on the Kombi. It came in a single colour but, for a little extra, purchasers could buy it in two-tone. It still encapsulated basic camping – without the tent – but allowed the Camper more room with its more basic, nine-litre water tank (compared to the former Mark III) with one table and the obligatory Easicool units. The floor space was bigger than in previous conversions due mainly to the decrease in furniture. Gone were the finely-tuned wooden constructions from JP White although it came in much cheaper and was an affordable option for the masses. In the same year, the Caravette was also developed and despite being a more expensive purchase never failed to woo buyers with its hidden extras. In 1962, the most notable extension to this flamboyant roadster was its most exciting innovation in the form of a fibre-glass elevated ceiling which allowed more than six foot from floor to roof. It allowed the vehicle to be utilised to the full and was Devon's own answer to the Dormobile which was taking the camping world by storm.

Known as the Gentlux, it came as a pop-up top roof with a fitted skylight. Today it is hard to find any that survive from this time as it was discontinued within 12 months to make way for Devon's next enterprise. But in 1963, Devon were ready to introduce more sleeping and standing space and by now both the Devonette and the Caravette were available on either a Kombi or Microbus design. The Gentlux was replaced with a side-hinged elevating roof option and windows as designed by Martin Walter which were supplied by

◀ 1975 Devon Eurovette and Devonette brochure

Dormobile. It allowed optional bunks to be fitted and gave greater sleeping potential while standing room was elevated to six foot six inches. In addition a different type of tent was introduced, known as the Devon Drive Away Frame Tent, which allowed the

Camper to leave their possessions on site while they took the vehicle off travelling for the day. It gave holiday-makers more room for manoeuvre and ensured that they would come back to the same pitch at the end of a day's sightseeing. Three years later and Devon were once again prepared for change.

A new, improved version of the Devonette was flagged and aptly named the Torvette. It had an adaptable layout with a large floor space which gave the owner the option of utilising the vehicle for other purposes besides camping and travelling. The following year saw the introduction of the Spaceway, which could arguably be called the predecessor of the modern motorhome in that it allowed the driving seat and passenger seat to be connected to the living area. In today's sophisticated motorhomes it is possible to swivel the two or three seats in the cab to turn around and interface with the dinette and living accommodation. In the 1965, the Spaceway was slightly simpler but the idea was nonetheless the forerunner of this space-enhancing technology. What the Spaceway actually did was to allow the Caravette and Torvette models to be redesigned so that the interior lacked a bulkhead, but instead gave the front bench seat the option of being a single seat that held a storage locker underneath with a rear cushion that could be positioned against what would have been the bulkhead or side wall both for travelling or dining. In addition, Spaceways now incorporated an "awning" or canopy as standard on the side of the vehicle and purchasers were no longer encouraged to buy this optional extra.

◀ 1961 Devon Caravette brochure

However, it took until 1970 for Devon to launch their most famous conversion – the Moonraker. It was a complete redesign and makeover of the previous Caravettes, Devonettes and Torvettes based on the Kombi or Microbus. This innovative new model now incorporated the Caravette and Eurovette models and due to sheer enterprise and dedication to the mould, Devon became one of only three companies to ever gain official approval from VW Volkswagen and in 1972 they completed an exclusive deal that allowed all their conversions to be covered under a VW warranty and service.

This had been no mean feat and although it's not usual to see many VW Campers on a camp site today – motorhomes have become too prevalent – they enjoyed a renaissance during the 1980s and 1990s that still gives pleasure to people, whatever their reason for owning one may be.

Chapter 14

Other Conversions

Danbury

▶ 1969 Danbury conversion

WITH COMPETITIVE MARKETS abounding, Danbury, based in Essex, were undoubtedly leading the way in VW conversions. As a somewhat late arrival on the scene the company set to with gusto launching their Danbury Multicar in 1964 which was based on the VW models from the previous year. The company found an unusual approach to their conversions and were dedicated to the convenience of the vehicle they found favour with. It was described by many as a vehicle first and foremost, but was also championed as a "comfortable motor caravan" by Autocar. It was based on the early Panel Van as well as the Kombi and Microbus and came with loading doors on both sides which was fairly unusual. These had to be specified at the time of order on Panel Van conversions but the Kombi conversions by Danbury were to prove more popular with punters.

There was a bench seat that ran down one side for use in the daytime and the table was separately stored under the roof locker above the engine, but when in use, had two legs which could also enable the table to be used as a stand-alone unit outside the vehicle and had the option of extra beds for adults in addition to the two adults, two children scenario by having adult bunks in the main living area. All the fittings were detachable and the curtains were contained on one continuous rail that meant that they could be tucked away at the back should the traveller opt for more of a vehicle than a Camper when driving.

As with many other conversions, cutlery and crockery were supplied as

OOR 415G

1968 Danbury brochure

standard and were stowed away in storage spaces built especially for the purpose.

Two years later and some minor amendments were made in re-design where walk-through models became standard and the spare wheel could be mounted on the front of the vehicle to maximise space. In addition, a cleverly concealed "middle" seat could be positioned between the cab and the living area to provide extra day-time seating and the new design came fully fitted with a Danbury Ridge Tent which was essentially a free-standing awning that, like other conversions, meant that Campers could off load their possessions and supplies and leave them at the camping site on their pitch while they drove off to explore their surroundings. It made camping and space more flexible and provided users with more accommodation than would be normal within the confines of the Camper alone. By now, electric mains hook-ups were available as optional extras – something Campers today take for granted.

▶ 1978 Eurec Cassandra brochure

Four years after their exciting arrival, Danbury began marketing the new shaped Danbury with bay windows, where the focus was very much aimed at providing a multi-use vehicle that was designed for travelling as well as offering overnight accommodation, and the seats were all forward-facing. Like the Devon, Danbury was one of the three VW approved converters between the late 1960s and 1972. The company lost out to their rivals when Devon signed an exclusive deal with VW although they regained their position in 1977. During the early 2000s, Danbury made a high-profile comeback when conversion company, Beetles UK, bought the name to fit in with the conversion of Type 2 buses into Campers. There are currently two versions of the Danbury available today which combine the charm and looks of the 1960s model with modern technology to be found in any motorhome.

Eurec Campers

AS COMPANIES SUCH AS DORMOBILE and Westfalia kept the VW Camper in the limelight, Devon continued its reign in the UK with its conversions such as the Eurovette and the Devon 21, as well as the Sundowner and T25 models, which sported a newer squarer frontage. Meanwhile, other companies with VW conversions were taking off and, in 1978, Holland introduced a new style of Camper to the rest of the continent in the Eurec Camper which was available in two models.

Cassandra and the Pandora, the former comprised of a cooker, fridge, storage and sink down the inside while the sliding door heralded a fold-down "buddy" seat. The Pandora, on the other hand, had a swing-out cooker and sink that sat snugly at the end of the bench while both had full-length side-hinged elevating roofs.

They were largely based on Devon models and catered for the Ben Pon dealership clientele while the Devon and Ben Pon relationship continued its ground-breaking legacy. Initially, Eurec Campers were mainly constructed on the Devon Moonraker and were made left-hand drive.

This continued when the T25 range became prevalent although the fact that Devon had supplied the vehicles for conversion was left out of the marketing and badges.

▲ 1978 Viking conversion

EZ Campers

ANOTHER PROLIFIC CONVERSION company at the time was EZ, a US company based in California. There, with insight and intuition, the company knew that demand far outstripped supply and began converting panel vans in the early 1960s. EZ conversions were varied though as the company also offered a service to consumers who owned VW 211 vans which could also be converted for holidays and travelling. Closely modelled on the Westfalia interior, the EZ VW 211 conversions were renamed El Viajero – meaning the traveller – and were renowned for their practicality and versatility.

Holdsworth Conversions

THEN CAME THE HOLDSWORTH. A prolific conversion company based in

Middlesex and which didn't begin working on VW Campers until the late 1960s. Having gained a reputation for reputable conversions, the company moved to Reading where they were able to work on up to 15 VW Camper conversions at any one time. Holdsworth were responsible for the full-length elevating roof design which came in two options including the Weathershield – a pop-top concertina style roof and became synonymous with bay windows and hard-wearing upholstery. The company went on to win many awards for their innovative designs and good quality.

Viking

DESPITE ALL THE BIG NAMES associated with conversions, which are in reality too numerous to cover, Viking must surely be worth a mention. One of the main features that makes this Camper stand out from all others is the fully elevating roof, as opposed to the side-hinged roof which only lifts on one side. The elevating roof not only gave more headroom to the vehicle's occupants, but also allowed a more roomy feel to the overall layout which was to prove exceptionally popular with purchasers and critics alike. The roof is, quite simply huge, and elevates to such a position that even adults can sleep comfortably up "in the roof" without fear of claustrophobia or being cramped.

It was initially launched in 1970 at the height of the VW Camper conversions and was, like many other great names in the business, produced in the UK by Motorhomes based in Hertfordshire. The first models comprised a fixed roof and had an optional pop top which was elevated from the mid to rear section of the vehicle. It had a spacious interior – despite the lack of roof space to begin with – and could comfortably seat four or five diners around the table with its facing bench seating. The Viking also marked a first in that it offered a sound system – a Philips stereo cassette system – as standard. There was also a cab hammock available for sleeping that one extra person and came with the optional extra of an Isabella awning – again, a stand-alone "tent" that could be left behind during the day, which was capable of sleeping up to three further people.

Sadly, due to politics and in-fighting the Viking came under scrutiny when

Modifications come in many shapes and sizes as shown with this unusual demountable Camper

VW GB claimed that its elevated roof was a serious concern because it lacked the relevant roof strengthening. Motorhomes immediately hit back and challenged the UK-based company to substantiate its claims. Marketing was seen as the most likely scenario for the unprecedented attack and VW GB's claims were quickly dismissed by the media and the Viking's adoring public at large. Indeed, it went on to become one of the most sought-after elevating roof conversions of its time.

There was never any evidence to the contrary that the Viking was a

individual customers. After high profile dominance on the scene for more than 20 years, Viking closed down its operations in the mid-1980s having spearheaded the innovation in VW Camper conversions. Today, these long-established vehicles are highly sought after and greatly treasured by those who own them.

phenomenal vehicle with a good safety record and the Motorhomes company went on to launch the Viking Spacemaker and the roof became a camping fraternity must-have. It became a huge selling point for the company, and many other VW conversions, including Devons, were eventually fitted with Viking roofs for

Chapter 15

The Culture

▶ Camper Vans have become a lifestyle for many people

FOR MANY, VW CAMPERS AND SURFERS go hand-in-hand, but there seems very little to suggest why this should have happened, other than that both were in the right place at the right time. As the surfing culture grew from the late 1950s onwards and into the mid-1960s, the VW Camper conversions were gaining in popularity with various different groups in society, most notably those with a surfboard stuck permanently under one arm – unless they were in the sea, of course. Campers and surfers became symbols of a relaxed, carefree lifestyle that was epitomised by the roaring of waves and the humming of the boxed-in rear engine. That the two suited each other there can be no doubt.

The Camper gave the surfer a place to keep his board and somewhere to stay when he travelled to the coast in pursuit of his other passion. The VW became a convenient and ever-faithful mode of

Coca-Cola

▲ The surf culture goes hand in hand with that of the Camper Van

transport even if it could overheat due to its air-cooled engine finding the travelling hard going. But surfers weren't just satisfied with surfing the sea, they developed the idea of the skateboard so they could continue their activities on land. In turn, the VW followed and began another lengthy and extraordinary relationship with another culture-crazed enthusiast, the skateboarder. This in time developed to include snowboarders too and it's still a cherished vehicle for all three. Surfers have remained loyal to the VW Camper for almost 40 years, and judging by the numbers who still turn up in them by the beach, there seems to be no sign of the love affair abating anytime soon.

▶ Custom designs are common place with Camper Van restorations

1966
827 DKQ 91
VOLKSWAGEN

Chapter 16

Clubs, Shows & Rallies

Vanfest

▶ Early and late Bay Westies on show

SINCE 1994 VANFEST HAS BEEN drawing in record numbers of crowds to what is the world's largest VW Transporter event in the annual calendar. Held in September each year, the event attracts enthusiasts from all over the globe who are keen to experience what organisers, VANFEST Ltd and the Volkswagen Type 2 Owners Club have in store. In 2006, the event saw more than 5,000 vehicles descend on the Three Counties Showground, near Malvern in Worcestershire. The ground offers an array of facilities including extensive camping and large halls which cater for those attending when the weather decides to be less than kind. For those camping, electric hook-ups are only available for disabled and special needs vans so these are limited, but the site also boasts a restaurant and many mobile vans offering food and refreshments as well as basic provisions.

There are around 250 trade and craft stalls and Vanfest also has an extremely popular sales area where enthusiasts can purchase the vehicle of their dreams. Most have come to see the older type transporters and these are displayed in an arena where owners are encouraged to tell their tales of travel and excitement. There's even a specialist area for vans that have something a little bit different including different types of engines while Westfalia are well-

represented in the older type section. In September 2007, there was a special display celebrating 40 years of the Bay Window Transporter and at each Vanfest there is the chance for vehicles to win prizes. The Show & Shine, as with all other shows, is a highlight on Sunday and is definitely a must see while the weekend's entertainment features live bands which cater for families and younger enthusiasts alike.

The event is so huge that it provides a fun fair and a free crèche and has the unusual approach of featuring "Cooking in a Camper," where audiences are kept captivated by creative ways in which to cook up a storm in a VW Transporter. This ends with an annual "Cook Off" competition in the show ring. The event's exceptional reputation and sheer size and capacity require a huge amount of preparation, which begins almost as soon as the current show is coming to a close.

The week before Vanfest there is a huge show build-up. Although it's

GINSTERS
Cornish
THROUGH AND THROUGH
www.ginsters.co.uk
GINSTERS
Cornish
THROUGH AND THROUGH
REAL HON

◀ Customised Ginsters Van 2007

mainly about the VW's there are also many other attractions and things to do throughout the weekend which only add to the excitement. Saturday night also includes a pig roast. Despite its size and the crowds that flock to Vanfest it is a warm and friendly weekend for all the family.

Run To The Sun

NEWQUAY, THE SURF CAPITAL OF the UK, is usually awash with VW Camper vans at the height of summer. It's probably fair to say that most of the year round old faithfuls turn up in their humming vehicles and park by the sea ready to catch the next wave.

But more than this, the seaside resort is swamped in May each year by the huge numbers of VW enthusiasts who make their way from Reading services on the M4 and travel in convoy down the M5 before hitting the A30 on the home-stretch towards Cornwall. This particular part of the festivities, known as the cruise, is organised by *Volksworld* magazine and heralds the start of the weekend.

What's it all about? Run To The Sun, or RTTS as its affectionately known, is a cult rally that sees masses of people

▶ 1960 Samba, with miniature replica

travelling in their VW Campers on their way to a three-day event extravaganza on the Cornish Riviera where there's the opportunity to meet up with old friends and like-minded people who share the same passions – sun, sea, surf and VWs. The 2007 event was a massive success where literally thousands descended on Trevelgue Holiday Park for a well-deserved weekend of mayhem. It was RTTS's 21st birthday and even the rain on the second day did little to dampen spirits.

There are four arenas set up for entertainment throughout the weekend, but surely the travelling must be an important part of the VW bug? There were live bands, comedians and a 1970s disco which all added to the hype while the "Show n' Shine" held on the Saturday is a highlight which attracted more than 300 competitors with their cars, and more than 25,000 spectators. The custom is for Volksworld magazine, along with other judges, to pick out 10 winners. Previous events have seen the likes of Marco V, Plump DJ's, Lisa Lashes, Tidy Boys, Kenny Ken, Nick Warrn and Mark Hamilton heading for the coastal resort while the main event is organised by Cranstar Event Management in Newquay.

▲ Showfield at the Camper Van rally

The festival was inspired by the car/Camper beach culture and the traditional surfer's love of the VW which quickly established itself as the preferred mode of transport. Launched in 1987, the first RTTS attracted around 70 cars while today the numbers are rising year on year and an estimated 100,000 people are thought to have attended the event in 2007. Many of them have travelled from the far reaches of the UK or beyond to attend.

VW Festival

SET IN THE GROUNDS OF HARE-HOUSE, Leeds, this prestigious event is aimed at anyone wanting to show off their prized VW car or Van. It's a show that's definitely all about the Dubs and is promoted as a great day out for all the family. Like RTTS, there's a "Show n' Shine" where enthusiasts can admire those vehicles that have been kept in good nick, while it's also possible to wander around the historic Harewood House itself taking in the art collections then head back outside to stroll around the famous Bird Garden and hop in a boat for a trip across the lake. There's also an adventure playground for the younger members of the family who might like a little more challenge and excitement and the festival offers live bands as well as an extensive programme of events and exhibitions.

For those wishing to camp over the whole weekend (note the festival is only open on the Sunday) there are 70 pitches available at nearby Haighfield Caravan Park. Camping is also available at Harewood House itself but is aimed primarily at "quieter" Campers and those with families and has been run on a trial basis to see whether a two-day event would be possible. The VW Festival was born when a trio of enthusiasts decided that a VW event that didn't focus on the Midlands was a pre-requisite in the calendar. Although only in its third year, the VW Festival has proved a massive success with those in the north and provides the main component of that VW event – the cars. The "Show "n" Shine" has proved since 2005 to be a big crowd-puller and the Festival's organisers are looking forward to their fourth event next year. Perhaps the camping in the grounds this year will have helped and maybe a two-day event is in the offing next time round.

Demon Dubs

MEETINGS OF THE DEMON DUBS promise a friendly Volkswagen meet for enthusiasts around Warrington and beyond. There are no rules, no fee and the only requirement is for a passion for all things VW. You don't even have to own a VW, you just have to love them. Demon Dubs meet every two weeks on a Sunday afternoon unless there's a VW show to go to. The club has its own website and offers news through its notice board and news announcements.

Weekender

THEY'RE EVEN DOING IT IN IRELAND. Camping takes place overlooking Ireland's only fjord at the Killary in Connemara. The facilities for Campers are extensive, but if you don't have a Van, then the nearby hostel built in the late 1800s has more than 100 rooms. The only thing the organisers ask is that those attending are prepared for a weekend of VW.

▶ A classic
Postal Panel Van

TSCHE BUNDESPOST

Chapter 17

CamperVantastic

THE VW CAMPERVAN HAS LONG been associated with 1960's and 1970's nostalgia, love and peace! But whatever your reason for loving these vehicles you've probably been drawn to them either from childhood campervan memories or a yearning for adventure.

My family and I were fortunate enough to take our first campervan on a road trip that took us to the shores of Sicily and Islands of Greece. As we travelled across Europe we relished the sheer beauty and magnitude of the changing landscape, which is completely lost when travelling by air. We had an incredible journey and while we were on the road we developed our ideas for CamperVantastic.

Whether you buy one or hire one you'll always meet people who want one. Classic

or new there is a VW campervan for you, whatever your dream, be it family holidays, festival action, romantic breaks, surf trips or just escaping the humdrum and hitting the open road.

The VW California campervan brings campervanning into the 21st Century and offers a truly independent 'glamping' experience. At CamperVantastic we've assisted many a happy camper to discover remote and idyllic places and windswept beaches! So we hope you have enjoyed flicking through these pages looking at some of the best campervans around and if you're not one already, we're confident you'll soon become a camperfan!

Steve Lumley,
Director, CamperVantastic
www.campervantastic.com

The pictures in this book were provided courtesy of the following:

GETTY IMAGES
101 Bayham Street, London NW1 0AG

David Eccles

VW Camper and Commercial Magazine
www.volkswagencamper.co.uk

Photo courtesy of Ginsters
www.ginsters.co.uk

Distributed in association with G2 Entertainment Limited